Map Skills for Today

Grade 4

Traveling Near and Far

Map Skills for Today
Traveling Near and Far
Grade 4

Publisher: Keith Garton
Editorial Director: Maureen Hunter-Bone
Editorial Development: Summer Street Press, LLC
Writer: Jessica Rudolph
Project Editor: Miriam Aronin
Editor: Alex Giannini
Design and Production: Dinardo Design, LLC
Photo Editor: Kim Babbitt

Illustration Credits: Stephanie Powers
Map Credits: Mapping Specialists, Ltd.
Photo Credits: Page 4: Jupiter Images; Page 5: Corbis, John Klein/Weekly Reader; Page 9: Photos.com;
Page 11: Photos.com; Page 17: Photos.com; Page 19: Jupiter Images; Page 20: AP Photo/Tomas van Houtryve;
Page 21 & 24: Jupiter Images; Page 29: Jupiter Images; Page 30: AP Images; Page 33: Jupiter Images;
Page 36: Wonderfile; Page 38: Jupiter Images; Page 39: Photos.com; Page 40: Corbis; Page 41: AP Images

Teachers: Go online to www.scholastic.com/mapskillsfortoday for teaching ideas and the answer key.

ISBN: 978-1-338-21491-8

3 4 5 6 7 8 9 10   40   23 22 21 20

Traveling Near and Far

Table of Contents

The World We Live In

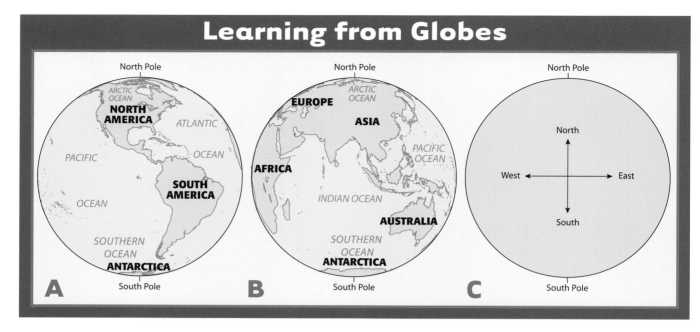

Learning from Globes

For a long time, people thought Earth was flat. But around 500 B.C., the Greeks learned that our planet is round. Have you ever used a globe to locate something on Earth? A globe is a round model of Earth. Globes give the most accurate picture of Earth as a whole. Only a globe can show the true shapes of land areas and bodies of water.

Globes show the Earth's oceans and continents. **Oceans** are Earth's largest bodies of water. **Continents** are its largest land areas. Globe A shows four oceans and three continents. What are they? Globe B shows five continents and four oceans. Can you name them?

Globes can help us learn about **directions** too. All directions on Earth are based on two important points.

These are the North Pole and the South Pole. Look at the arrows on Globe C. One arrow points toward the North Pole, the most northern point on Earth. This direction is north. South is the direction toward the South Pole, the most southern point on Earth. As you face north, east is to your right, and west is to your left. If you face south, east is to your left.

The ancient Greeks figured out that the world was round by studying the stars.

Aristotle lived in ancient Greece and came up with arguments that proved Earth was round.

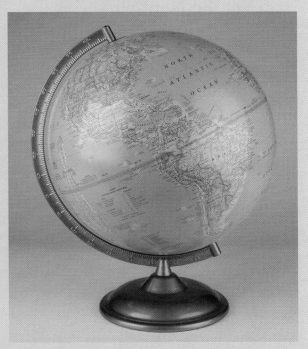

This is a classroom globe. The Greeks made the first globes to represent Earth.

Think It Over

Why do you think a globe is more accurate than a flat map?

✦ Use Your Skills

1. A _____ is a model of Earth.

2. The four main directions are _____ , _____ , _____ , and _____ .

3. The most northern point on Earth is called the _____ .

4. The _____ Ocean is north of North America.

5. The South Pole is located on the continent of _____ .

6. Which ocean is surrounded by Africa, Asia, and Australia? _____

Complete each sentence with *north*, *south*, *east*, or *west*.

7. South America is _____ of Antarctica.

8. If you were facing north, you would turn right to face _____ .

9. Europe is located to the _____ of Asia.

10. The continent of Australia is _____ of Africa.

👉 Your Turn Now

Use the library or the Internet to learn more about the ancient Greeks. How did they study Earth and the stars? Create a poster that shows how the Greeks made scientific discoveries.

Locating Ourselves in the World

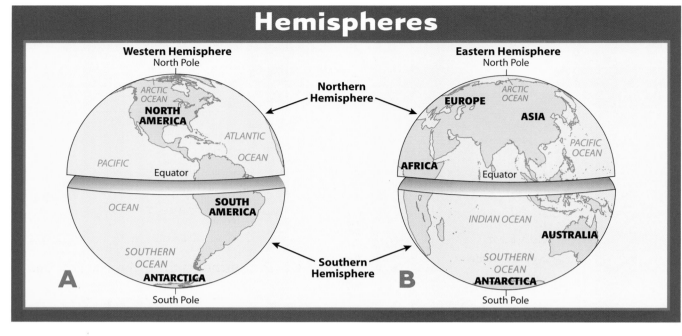

Hemispheres

The **equator** is an imaginary line that divides the globe into two equal parts. Each half of the Earth is called a **hemisphere.** The Northern Hemisphere is north of the equator. The Southern Hemisphere is south of the equator. Mapmakers often show Eastern and Western Hemispheres as well. Globe A shows the Western Hemisphere. Globe B shows the Eastern Hemisphere. What continents are in each hemisphere?

Two sets of imaginary lines on globes are used to measure distances on Earth. One set runs east to west. These are called lines of **latitude.** They are parallel lines. That means they never come together. Look at Globe C on page 7 to see the lines of latitude. The equator is a special line of latitude called 0°. Latitude measures distance north or south of the equator in degrees (°). The North Pole is one of the points farthest from the equator. It is located at 90° North. The South Pole is at 90° South.

Another set of imaginary lines runs north to south. These are called lines of **longitude.** They come together at the North and South Poles. You can see these lines on Globe D. Longitude measures distance east and west, from 0° to 180° in each direction. The line 0° longitude has a special name. It is called the prime meridian. The **prime meridian** is the starting point for measuring longitude. Look at Globe E to find both sets of lines.

Latitude and Longitude

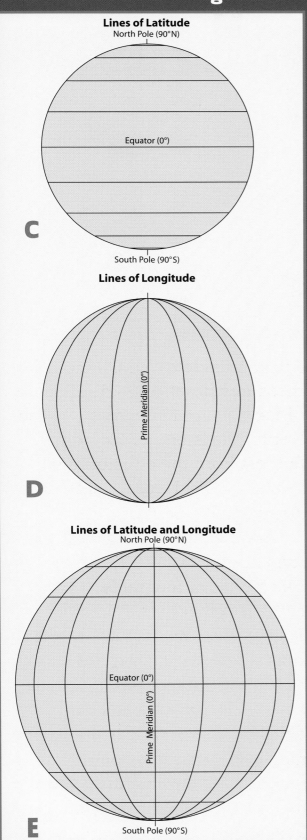

Lines of Latitude

North Pole (90°N)

Equator (0°)

South Pole (90°S)

C

Lines of Longitude

Prime Meridian (0°)

D

Lines of Latitude and Longitude

North Pole (90°N)

Equator (0°)

Prime Meridian (0°)

South Pole (90°S)

E

Use Your Skills

1. All the lines that run north to south come together at the _____ .

2. Lines of _____ never come together.

3. The Earth is divided into the Northern and Southern Hemispheres by the _____ .

4. Which continents does the equator pass through? _____ _____

5. The _____ is the starting point for measuring longitude.

6. South America is in the Northern, Southern, and _____ Hemispheres.

7. Most of Asia is _____ of the equator.

8. _____ and _____ are the only continents completely in the Southern Hemisphere.

Think It Over

Why do you think mapmakers divide the Earth into hemispheres?

Mapping Our Country

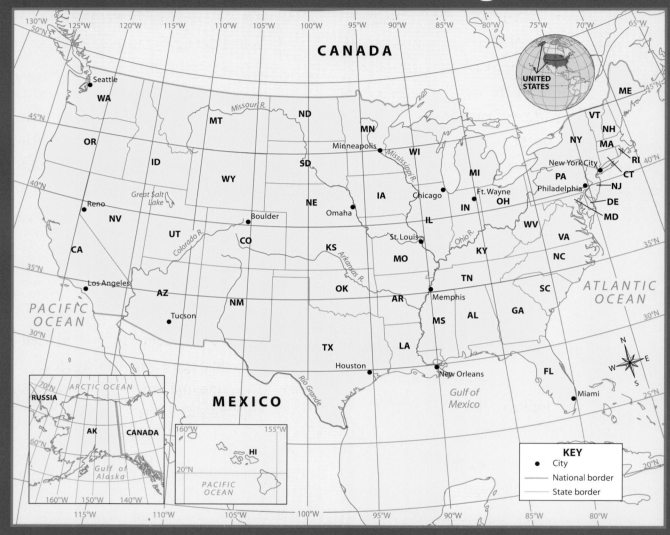

United States, Latitude and Longitude

Flat maps can tell us more about a smaller part of Earth than globes can. The map above shows the United States. Directions are shown by a **compass rose**, with arrows facing north, east, south, and west.

The map above includes a locator globe and inset maps. A **locator globe** is a small globe that has the main map area highlighted.

This locator globe shows where the United States is located on Earth.

An **inset map** is a small map within a larger map that can show details not seen on the larger map. The inset maps above show Alaska and Hawaii. These states are not connected to the mainland United States.

Using Latitude and Longitude

The map on page 8 shows latitude and longitude, just like on a globe. Here, latitude and longitude are shown every 5 degrees. The United States is north of the equator, so all lines of latitude on this map are north latitudes. The United States is also west of the prime meridian, so all lines of longitude are west longitudes.

Let's say you want to describe the location of a place such as Houston, Texas. Find the closest line of latitude and the closest line of longitude. The closest lines to Houston are 30° North latitude and 95° West longitude. When describing a location, give the latitude first and abbreviate the direction. So, Houston is located at about 30°N, 95°W.

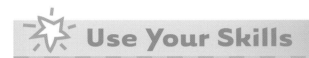 **Use Your Skills**

1. A _____ shows directions on a map.

2. A small map that shows details is called an _____ .

3. Fort Wayne, Indiana, lies on which line of longitude? _____

4. Which three states does the 30°N latitude line run through?

   _____ , _____ , and _____

5. What are the closest lines of latitude and longitude to Philadelphia?

   _____

6. Describe the approximate location of New Orleans, Louisiana.

   _____

7. What city is located at about 40°N, 120°W?

   _____

 **Map It!**

Find your community on a map of the country or your state. Then draw a dot showing where your community is located on the map on page 8. Find the nearest lines of latitude and longitude. Using these lines, describe where your town or city is located.

New York City is the largest city in the United States. Its location in the world is 41°N, 74°W.

Using Maps

Alaska, Map Symbols

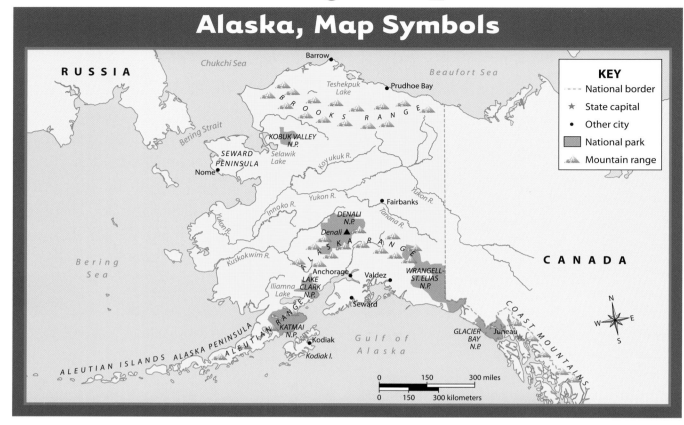

Many maps have symbols to help us better understand the map. A **symbol** is a line, drawing, or color that stands for something else. Certain map symbols are the same in most maps. For example, blue is usually used to show water. The border between countries or states may be shown by a broken line. An airport can be shown by an airplane shape, and a capital city by a star. Symbols are explained in a small box on the map called a **map key**. What symbols on the Alaska map are explained in the map key?

Many maps also include a map scale. A **map scale** is a line on a map that can help you figure out what a distance on a map equals in actual miles on Earth. Each inch on a map stands for a longer unit of distance—a mile, a hundred miles, or more.

On the map of Georgia on page 11, use a ruler to measure the map scale. One inch equals 100 miles. To find the distance between two points on the map, measure how many inches apart they are. Then multiply by the number of miles each inch equals. Suppose two places are three inches apart on the map of Georgia. That means they are really three times 100—or 300—miles apart.

Georgia, Small Scale Map

Tennessee

0 | 50 | 100 miles
0 | 50 | 100 kilometers

Athens

★ Atlanta

Augusta

South Carolina

Macon

Georgia

Alabama

Savannah

Chattahoochee River
Flint River
Ocmulgee River
Oconee River
Savannah River
Altamaha River
Flint River

ATLANTIC OCEAN

Florida

N
W E
S

Atlanta, Georgia, Large Scale Map

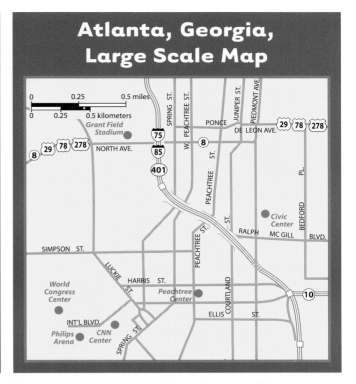

Different scales show different areas. A large area, like a state, uses a small scale. A smaller area, like a city, uses a large scale.

Use Your Skills

Use the maps on page 10 and on this page to answer the questions.

1. Alaska shares a national border with _____ .

2. A star represents the _____ of Alaska.

3. The small scale map on this page shows _____ . The large scale map shows _____ .

4. Atlanta is about _____ miles from Savannah.

5. It is about _____ miles from Grant Field Stadium to the Civic Center.

Think It Over

Why is it helpful for map symbols to look the same on different maps?

Your Turn Now

Create a map of the neighborhood around your school. Use at least five symbols in your map.

Downtown Atlanta, Georgia

Near the Water

Most maps show bodies of water. Compare the map and the terms below. Then look at the map of Europe on page 13. Which bodies of water can you see on the Europe map?

Terms—Bodies of Water

bay narrow part of an ocean or large lake that cuts into land

canal narrow waterway made by humans for ships to travel through

channel a body of water that joins two larger bodies of water

coast land at the edge of a large body of water

gulf an arm of an ocean or sea, usually larger than a bay

lake large body of water with land all or nearly all around it

ocean any of the five largest bodies of water on Earth

river large stream of water that empties into a lake, other river, sea, or ocean

sea large body of water somewhat smaller than an ocean

Bodies of Water

Europe, Bodies of Water

KEY
1 Czech Republic
2 Slovakia
3 Hungary
4 Austria
5 Switzerland
6 Slovenia
7 Croatia
8 Bosnia and Herzegovina
9 Serbia
10 Kosovo
11 Montenegro
12 Albania
13 Macedonia
14 Moldova
15 Russia
16 Lithuania
17 Latvia
18 Estonia
19 Belgium
20 Netherlands
21 Denmark

Use Your Skills

1. What four seas border Italy?_____

_____

_____

2. What body of water separates the United Kingdom and France?_____

_____

3. What sea borders both Europe and Africa?_____

4. Name two gulfs and one bay off the European continent. _____

_____

5. The Seine River is in what country?

_____

6. Which countries does the Dnieper River flow through?_____

_____

Map It!

On the map on page 13, draw a line along the shortest water route from Portugal to Sweden. Which bodies of water does your route include?

On the Land

A map can show many different types of landforms. Compare these terms to the art below. Then look at the map of the United States on page 15. Which landforms can you see on the map of the United States?

Terms—Landforms

canyon steep, narrow valley with high sides

desert very dry land

forest area of land where many trees grow

hill rounded land higher than the land around it

island land with water all around it

mountain a very tall hill; a long row of mountains is a *mountain range*

peak pointed top of a mountain

peninsula land with water on three sides

plain very large area of flat land

plateau high, wide area of flat land, with steep sides

valley low land between mountains or hills

Landforms

Mountain
Peak
Valley
Plateau
Desert
Canyon
Hill
Plain
Peninsula
Island
Forest

United States, Landforms

 Use Your Skills

Write whether each statement is *true* or *false*.

1. The Rocky Mountains pass through Wyoming (WY) and Colorado (CO). _____

2. Brooks Range lies in Arizona (AZ). _____

3. The Adirondack Mountains are east of Lake Ontario. _____

4. The Appalachian Mountains are located in several states in the eastern part of the country. _____

5. The Arkansas River runs through the Ouachita Mountains. _____

6. The Ozark Plateau lies in the Rocky Mountains. _____

7. The Coastal Plain includes the state of Minnesota (MN). _____

 **Your Turn Now**

Do research to find out how tall these mountains are: Mt. Whitney, Denali, Mauna Kea, Pikes Peak, and Mt. Rainier. Make a graph to compare their heights.

Exploring North America

North America, Political

ASIA
RUSSIA

ARCTIC OCEAN

ICELAND

GREENLAND
(Denmark)

Bering Sea

Beaufort Sea

Baffin Bay

Davis Strait

UNITED STATES
(Alaska)

Labrador Sea

CANADA

Hudson Bay

Gulf of St.Lawrence

Great Lakes

Ottawa

Mississippi R.

UNITED STATES

Washington,D.C.

ATLANTIC OCEAN

PACIFIC OCEAN

Gulf of Mexico

BAHAMAS

DOMINICAN REPUBLIC

MEXICO

Havana

CUBA

Santo Domingo

PUERTO RICO
(U.S.)

HAITI

Port-au-Prince

Mexico City

JAMAICA

Kingston

Belmopan

BELIZE

Caribbean Sea

HONDURAS

Guatemala

Tegucigalpa

NORTH AMERICA

GUATEMALA

San Salvador

Managua

NICARAGUA

EL SALVADOR

PANAMA

San Jose

SOUTH AMERICA

Panama

CENTRAL AMERICA

COSTA RICA

N
NW NE
W E
SW SE
S

Equator

KEY
⊛ National capital
— National border

0   500   1,000 miles
0   500   1,000 kilometers

We live on the continent of North America. North America includes Canada, the large island of Greenland, the United States, and Mexico. It also includes the countries in Central America and many island nations in the Caribbean Sea.

The compass rose on the map of North America has four main directions—north, south, east, and west. These are called **cardinal directions**. This compass rose includes intermediate directions as well. **Intermediate directions** are halfway between two cardinal directions. On a compass, NE stands for *northeast*; SE for *southeast*; NW for *northwest*; and SW for *southwest*.

The Rocky Mountains cover much of western North America, from Canada through the United States.

⭐ Use Your Skills

Look at the map on page 16. Fill in the blanks with intermediate directions: *NE, SE, NW*, and *SW*.

1. Alaska is _____ of Cuba.

2. Greenland is _____ of Hudson Bay.

3. Jamaica is _____ of Honduras.

4. Puerto Rico is _____ of the Bahamas.

5. Mexico is _____ of Greenland.

6. The Caribbean Sea is _____ of the United States.

7. The Gulf of Mexico is _____ of South America.

👆 Your Turn Now

Choose a part of North America you would like to learn more about. Find and print photographs of it from the Internet. With your classmates, create a bulletin board about North America.

Our Neighbor, Canada

Canada, Major Highways

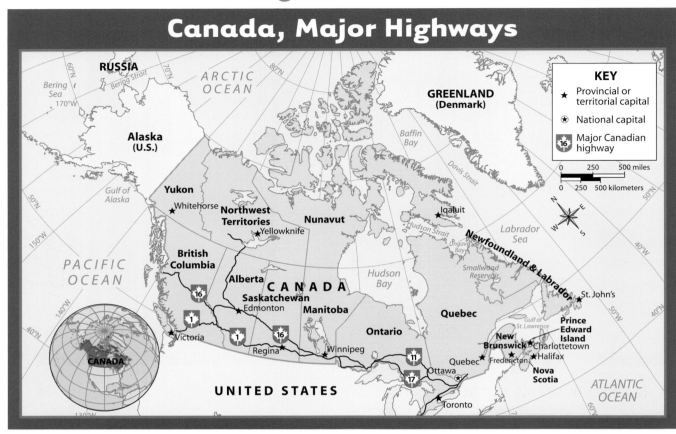

Canada is the second largest country in area in the world, after Russia. However, its **population**, or the number of people living there, is only the 38th largest. Canada and the United States share a border that is more than 5,000 miles long. Canada is divided into 13 smaller areas: 10 provinces and three territories. The map above uses this symbol 🍁 to mark Canada's major highway routes.

Use Your Skills

1. Which U.S. state does the Yukon Territory border? _____

2. What is Canada's easternmost province?

_____

3. Which two main routes would you take to get from Regina to Winnipeg?

_____

_____

Think It Over

In which part of the country are Canada's major highways located? What might this tell you about where most people in Canada live?

Our Neighbor, Mexico

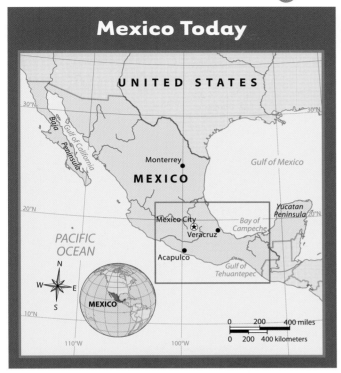

Mexico Today

UNITED STATES

MEXICO

Monterrey

Mexico City
Veracruz

Acapulco

Gulf of Mexico

Yucatan Peninsula

Bay of Campeche

Gulf of Tehuantepec

PACIFIC OCEAN

Baja Peninsula

Gulf of California

MEXICO

N W E S

0   200   400 miles
0   200   400 kilometers

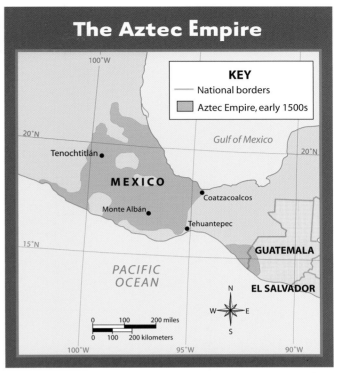

The Aztec Empire

KEY
— National borders
▨ Aztec Empire, early 1500s

Tenochtitlán

MEXICO

Monte Albán

Coatzacoalcos

Tehuantepec

Gulf of Mexico

PACIFIC OCEAN

GUATEMALA

EL SALVADOR

N W E S

0   100   200 miles
0   100   200 kilometers

Mexico is south of the United States. It also borders the Gulf of Mexico and the Pacific Ocean. Find Mexico City on the map of Mexico today. It is the capital of Mexico.

In the 1400s, a group of Native Americans called the Aztecs ruled a huge empire. It was located in what is today central and southern Mexico. Look at the map of the Aztec Empire to see what areas it once covered.

Aztec ruins can still be seen today in Mexico City.

Use Your Skills

Use both maps on this page to answer these questions.

1. The city of Veracruz is on what body of water?_____

2. The city of Acapulco is on what body of water?_____

3. The Aztec capital of Tenochtitlán was located in the same place as what city today?_____

Map It!

On the map of Mexico today, outline the borders of the Aztec Empire. What cities does this area include?

Exploring Central America

Central America, Political

MEXICO

BELIZE
★ Belmopan
Gulf of Honduras

GUATEMALA
Guatemala ★

PACIFIC OCEAN

HONDURAS
Tegucigalpa ★
Rio Coco

★ San Salvador
EL SALVADOR
Gulf of Fonseca

NICARAGUA

Caribbean Sea

Managua ★
Lake Nicaragua

KEY
— National boundary
★ National capital

0   50   100 miles
0   50   100 kilometers

COSTA RICA
★ San Jose

Gulf of Mosquitos

Coronado Bay

Panama Canal
★ Panama

PANAMA

Gulf of Panama

SOUTH AMERICA

N W E S

CENTRAL AMERICA

Ships carry products from around the world through the Panama Canal.

Central America is the farthest south region of North America. Its farthest south country is Panama. Panama is an **isthmus**, or a narrow strip of land, bordered on both sides by water, that connects two larger bodies of land. The Panama Canal, shown on the map above, was built by the United States and opened in 1914. It greatly reduced the distance ships had to travel when carrying goods between the Atlantic and Pacific Oceans.

Use Your Skills

Circle the answer for each question.

1. How many countries are there in Central America?

   a five   b seven   c nine

2. What body of water helps form the border between Honduras and Nicaragua?

   a Panama Canal   b Rio Coco
   c Pacific Ocean

3. Which country does not border the Gulf of Honduras?

   a Belize   b Guatemala
   c Costa Rica

Exploring South America

KEY
- ⊞ Amazon rain forest
- ✪ National capital
- ▲ Mountain peak

Caribbean Sea

Caracas ✪
VENEZUELA **GUYANA**
Bogotá ✪ Georgetown ✪ Paramaribo ✪
COLOMBIA **SURNAME** Cayenne ✪
Quito ✪ **FRENCH GUIANA (FRANCE)**
ECUADOR Amazon R. Equator
PERU **BRAZIL**
Lima ✪
ANDES MOUNTAINS La Paz ✪ Brasília ✪
BOLIVIA
Sucre ✪
PARAGUAY
Asunción ✪
CHILE **ARGENTINA**
Mt. Aconcagua ▲ **URUGUAY**
Santiago ✪ Montevideo ✪
PACIFIC OCEAN Buenos Aires ✪

ATLANTIC OCEAN

ATLANTIC OCEAN

FALKLAND ISLANDS (U.K.)

N W E S

SOUTH AMERICA

0   500   1,000 miles
0   500   1,000 kilometers

South America is the fourth largest continent in the world. The Amazon River, in the north, is almost 4,000 miles long. The Amazon rain forest covers more than 2 million square miles and almost half of Brazil's total area. Mount Aconcagua, in Argentina, is the highest point on the continent—and in the Western Hemisphere!

⭐ Use Your Skills

Find the capitals of the countries below. Careful! One country has two capitals.

1. Brazil _____

2. Argentina _____

3. Colombia _____

4. Bolivia _____

5. Uruguay _____

👉 Your Turn Now

The Amazon rain forest is the home of millions of species. Research the Amazon rain forest. Then make a list of at least three plants, three animals, and three insects that can be found there.

The Amazon rain forest is the largest rain forest in the world.

Exploring Europe

Europe, Political

KEY

GERMANY EU member countries

UKRAINE Non-member countries

The European Union, or EU, is made up of 28 countries in Europe. The EU was created in 1957.

Its goal is to help European countries work together for peace and prosperity.

⭐ Use Your Skills

1. The _____ Sea separates the United Kingdom from Norway.

2. _____ and _____ are two capital cities that lie on islands in the Mediterranean Sea.

3. Berlin is about _____ miles from Vilnius.

4. This European country borders the Aegean Sea. _____

Note: The United Kingdom is scheduled to withdraw from the EU as of October 2019.

Exploring Asia

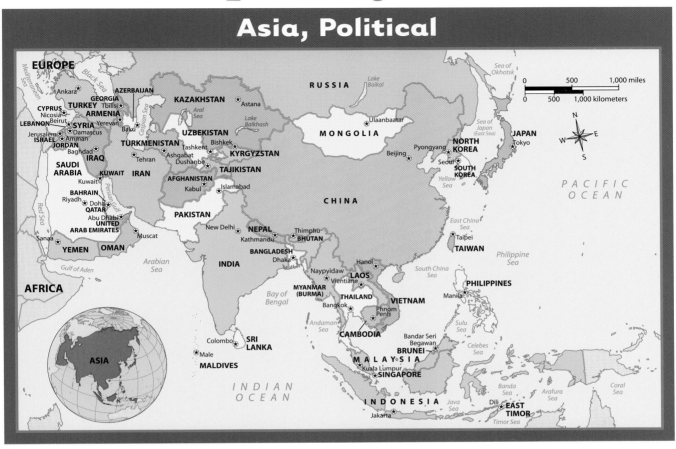

Asia, Political

Asia is the world's largest continent. It is home to both the highest and lowest points on Earth. The highest point is Mount Everest, which rises more than 29,000 feet. The lowest point is the Dead Sea, which is more than 1,000 feet below sea level.

Think It Over

Asia has two of the world's five largest countries in population. What challenges do you think this creates for the continent?

Use Your Skills

1. Asia is west of the _____ Ocean and north of the _____ Ocean.

2. The capital of Turkey is about _____ miles from the capital of China.

3. Israel borders the continent of _____ .

4. India, Bangladesh, and Myanmar border the Bay of _____ .

5. One Asian country that is made up of many islands is _____ .

Exploring Africa

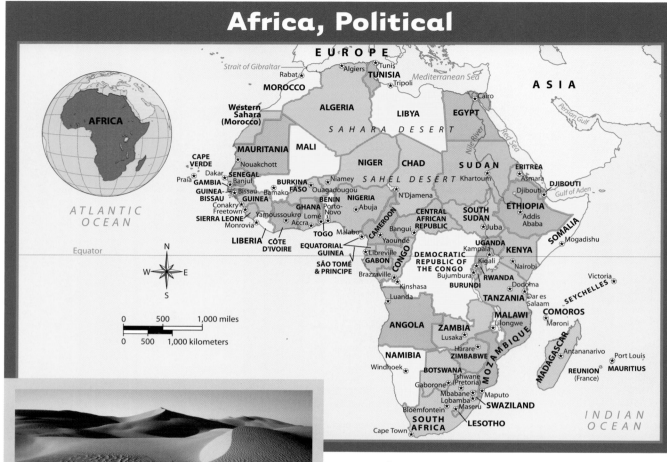

Africa, Political

EUROPE

Strait of Gibraltar
Rabat ✦
Algiers ✦ ✦Tunis
TUNISIA
✦Tripoli
Mediterranean Sea

ASIA

MOROCCO
✦Cairo
Persian Gulf

Western Sahara (Morocco)
ALGERIA
LIBYA
EGYPT

AFRICA

SAHARA DESERT
Nile River
Red Sea

MAURITANIA
MALI
NIGER
CHAD
SUDAN
ERITREA
✦Asmara
DJIBOUTI

CAPE VERDE
✦Nouakchott
Dakar✦
SENEGAL
SAHEL DESERT
Khartoum✦
✦Djibouti
Gulf of Aden

Praia
GAMBIA✦Banjul
Niamey✦
N'Djamena✦
ETHIOPIA
✦Addis Ababa
SOMALIA

GUINEA-BISSAU Bissau✦
BURKINA FASO
Ouagadougou✦
NIGERIA
✦Abuja

ATLANTIC OCEAN
Conakry✦ GUINEA
Bamako✦
BENIN
CENTRAL AFRICAN REPUBLIC
SOUTH SUDAN

Freetown✦
Yamoussoukro✦
Lomé✦Porto-Novo
Bangui✦
✦Juba
✦Mogadishu

SIERRA LEONE
Monrovia✦
Accra✦
GHANA
CAMEROON
Yaoundé✦
UGANDA
Kampala✦
KENYA

Equator
LIBERIA
CÔTE D'IVOIRE
TOGO
Malabo✦
EQUATORIAL GUINEA
✦Libreville
GABON
CONGO
DEMOCRATIC REPUBLIC OF THE CONGO
Kigali✦
RWANDA
✦Nairobi

N
W E
S
SÃO TOMÉ & PRINCIPE
Brazzaville✦
Bujumbura✦
BURUNDI
Dodoma✦
Victoria ✦

Kinshasa✦
TANZANIA
Dar es Salaam
SEYCHELLES

0 500 1,000 miles
Luanda✦
COMOROS

0 500 1,000 kilometers
ANGOLA
ZAMBIA
MALAWI
Lilongwe✦
✦Moroni

Lusaka✦
Harare✦
MOZAMBIQUE
MADAGASCAR
Antananarivo✦
✦Port Louis

NAMIBIA
ZIMBABWE
REUNION (France)
MAURITIUS

Windhoek✦
BOTSWANA
Tshwane (Pretoria)✦
Gaborone✦
Mbabane✦
Lobamba✦
✦Maputo

Bloemfontein✦
✦Maseru
SWAZILAND
INDIAN OCEAN

Cape Town✦
SOUTH AFRICA
LESOTHO

The Sahara Desert, in northern Africa, is the largest desert in the world.

Africa is the world's second largest continent. It covers nearly one-fifth of Earth's land surface. Africa is divided into two parts by the equator. Starting south of the equator and flowing north is the Nile River, the longest river in the world. The Nile stretches more than 4,000 miles. Many people live along the river's banks.

⭐ Use Your Skills

1. The capital of Ethiopia is _____.

2. _____ is the largest island nation of the African continent.

3. Morocco is separated from Europe by the Strait of _____.

4. The Sahara Desert and the _____ Desert are both _____ of the equator.

5. The equator passes through these six African countries: _____

_____.

Exploring Australia

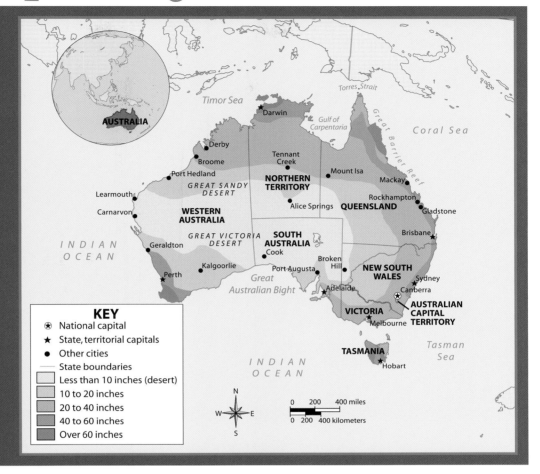

KEY
- ⊛ National capital
- ★ State, territorial capitals
- ● Other cities
- — State boundaries
- ☐ Less than 10 inches (desert)
- ☐ 10 to 20 inches
- ☐ 20 to 40 inches
- ☐ 40 to 60 inches
- ☐ Over 60 inches

Australia is the smallest continent on Earth. It is the only continent made up of just one country, also called Australia. It is separated into six states and two territories. Each one has its own capital.

Use Your Skills

1. Which Australian state is an island?

_____

2. The capital of Western Australia is

_____ .

3. Are more of Australia's cities located along the coast or inside the continent?

_____

4. The northern tip of Queensland receives more than _____ inches of rain yearly.

5. Does the Northern Territory receive more or less rainfall than South Australia?

_____

Think It Over

Why do you think most of Australia's cities are located in areas that receive larger amounts of rainfall?

25

All Fifty States

United States, Political

CANADA

WA
Olympia
Salem
OR
ID
Boise
Helena
MT
ND
Bismarck
MN
St. Paul
SD
Pierre
WI
Madison
MI
Lansing
Great Lakes
Superior
Huron
L. Michigan
Ontario
L. Erie
ME
Augusta
Montpelier
VT NH
Concord
Boston
Albany
MA
Providence
NY
Hartford
RI
CT

WY
Cheyenne
NE
Lincoln
IA
Des Moines
IL
Springfield
IN
Indianapolis
OH
Columbus
PA
Harrisburg
NJ
Trenton
Dover
MD
Annapolis
DE
Washington, D.C.

Sacramento
Carson City
Salt Lake City
Denver
CO
Topeka
KS
Jefferson City
MO
KY
Frankfort
WV
Charleston
Richmond
VA

NV
UT
UNITED STATES
Arkansas R.
Colorado R.
Great Salt Lake
Snake R.
Missouri R.
Mississippi R.

CA
AZ
Phoenix
Santa Fe
NM
Oklahoma City
OK
Little Rock
AR
Nashville
TN
NC
Raleigh
Columbia
SC
Atlanta
GA

PACIFIC OCEAN
ATLANTIC OCEAN

TX
Austin
MS
Jackson
AL
Montgomery
LA
Baton Rouge
Tallahassee
FL
Rio Grande

MEXICO
Gulf of Mexico

RUSSIA
AK
CANADA
Juneau
0   500 miles
0   500 kilometers

Honolulu
HI
0   200 miles
0   200 kilometers

0   250   500 miles
0   250   500 kilometers

KEY
⊛ National capital
★ State capital
— National border
— State border

Our country, the United States, is divided into fifty states. The map on this page shows all fifty states and their capitals. The map also shows Washington, D.C., our nation's capital. Which state do you live in? What is the capital of your state?

Think It Over

In order to travel to the national capital from your state, in which direction would you have to go?

Use Your Skills

Write the name of each state's capital city on the line.

1. Idaho _____

2. Colorado _____

3. Iowa _____

4. Kentucky _____

5. Florida _____

6. Arizona _____

7. Oregon _____

8. New York _____

A Growing Nation

United States, Population

KEY
- Few or no people
- Lightly settled
- Heavily settled
- Very heavily settled

Did you know that more than 300 million people live in the United States? However, some parts of the country have a larger population than other areas. The map on this page shows **population density**, or how many people live in a certain area. The colors tell you which places have few or many residents.

Use Your Skills

1. The light yellow color on this map stands for _____ .

   a few or no people　**b** lightly settled
   c heavily settled

2. A place that is red colored on the map is likely to have _____ cities.

   a few　　　**b** no　　　**c** many

3. A state that is more lightly settled than Texas is _____ .

   a New Mexico　　　**b** New York
   c California

4. Both the West Coast and the East Coast of the United States are _____ settled.

   a lightly　　　**b** heavily
   c moderately

5. A state that is more heavily settled than Nebraska is _____ .

   a Washington　　　**b** Montana
   c Wyoming

United States Regions

Regions of the United States

Sometimes it is helpful to divide a country into several regions. A **region** is an area of land with places that share similar features. The five regions of the United States are the Northeast, the Southeast, the Midwest, the Southwest, and the West.

 **Map It!**

Look at the chart on page 29. Then use a red crayon or marker to outline the region with the most land on the map on this page. In a different color, outline the largest state in each region.

Use Your Skills

1. The state of Maine is in what region?

   _____

2. The state of Michigan is in what region?

   _____

3. The state farthest south in the Southwest region is _____ .

4. Which two regions border the Gulf of Mexico? _____ and

   _____

5. California, Alaska, and Hawaii are part of the _____ region.

Facts about U.S. Regions

The Northeast
Area 191,678 square miles

Largest State: New York

The Southeast
Area 555,236 square miles

Largest State: Florida

The West
Area 1,576,336 square miles

Largest State: Alaska

The Midwest
Area 821,763 square miles

Largest State: Michigan

The Southwest
Area 572,784 square miles

Largest State: Texas

Use Your Skills

Use the map on page 28 and the chart on this page to answer the questions.

1. How many states are in each region?

_____

_____

_____

_____

2. Which two regions have the most states?

_____

3. Which region has the fewest states?

_____

4. Which region has the smallest land area?

_____

5. Which region has the largest land area?

_____

Millions of people live in New York City, in the Northeast region.

Your Turn Now

Using the Internet, find the U.S. state with the largest population. What is it? In which region is it? Why do you think this state has so many people?

The Northeast

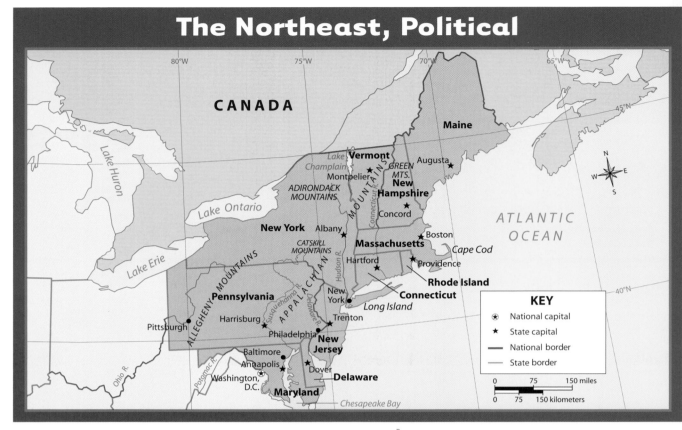

The Northeast, Political

CANADA

Maine

Vermont

Lake Champlain

Montpelier

GREEN MTS.

Augusta

ADIRONDACK MOUNTAINS

New Hampshire

Concord

Lake Ontario

New York

Albany

CATSKILL MOUNTAINS

Boston

Massachusetts

Cape Cod

Hartford

Providence

Lake Erie

ALLEGHENY MOUNTAINS

Hudson R.

Rhode Island

Connecticut

Pennsylvania

New York

Long Island

APPALACHIAN

Susquehanna R.

Delaware R.

Harrisburg

Trenton

Pittsburgh

Philadelphia

New Jersey

Ohio R.

Baltimore

Annapolis

Dover

Potomac R.

Washington, D.C.

Delaware

Maryland

Chesapeake Bay

ATLANTIC OCEAN

KEY

⊛ National capital
★ State capital
— National border
— State border

0   75   150 miles
0   75   150 kilometers

The Northeast region borders Canada to the north and the Atlantic Ocean to the east. It is the smallest region, but it has a large population. The climate of this region can include warm summers and winters with lots of snow. The map on page 31 shows average temperatures in the Northeast in the month of January.

A snowstorm in the Northeast

Use Your Skills

Write *true* or *false* on the line.

1. All the states in the Northeast border the Atlantic Ocean. _____

2. New York borders two Great Lakes. _____

3. Maine has a longer national border than Vermont. _____

4. Concord is the capital of Rhode Island. _____

5. Maine has a larger land area than Maryland. _____

Northeast, Average January Temperatures

C A N A D A

Maine

Vermont

New
Hampshire

Lake Huron

Lake Ontario

New
York

Massachusetts

ATLANTIC
OCEAN

Lake Erie

Rhode Island

Connecticut

Pennsylvania

KEY

Degrees Fahrenheit		Degrees Celsius
30° to 45°		-1° to 7°
15° to 30°		-9° to -1°
0° to 15°		-18° to -9°

New Jersey

Delaware

Maryland

Use Your Skills

1. Parts of which states have average January temperatures between 0°F and 15°F?

   _____

   _____

2. The average temperature in Rhode Island in January is between _____ and _____ degrees Fahrenheit.

3. Which state has the coldest average temperatures in January?

   _____

4. Which state has the warmest average temperatures in January?

   _____

Think It Over

In January, the Southeast averages temperatures between 30°F to more than 60°F. Do you think the Southeast is warmer or colder than the Northeast during the summer months?

Your Turn Now

Imagine you want to take a vacation in the Northeast region during January. Which state would you choose? What types of activities could you do?

The Southeast

The Southeast, Political

The Southeast borders the Atlantic Ocean to the east and the Gulf of Mexico to the south. The Mississippi River and other rivers help make the farmland fertile. Mild weather also makes this region ideal for growing a variety of crops.

A product map can help you learn about farming in the Southeast. The map on page 33 shows where certain crops and animals are raised in the region. Look at the map key. A picture of a cow is used to represent cattle. What other symbols are used?

Use Your Skills

1. Georgia is _____ of the Mississippi River.

2. The capital of West Virginia is about _____ miles from the capital of Florida.

3. The Southeastern state that extends farthest south is _____ .

4. The Southeastern states of _____ , _____ , _____ , and _____ border the Gulf of Mexico.

The Southeast, Agricultural Products

KEY

Cattle		Pigs	
Citrus fruit		Rice	
Corn		Sugarcane	
Cotton		Tobacco	
Peanuts		Soybeans	

Cotton is important to the economy of the Southeast region.

Your Turn Now

Peanuts are grown on many farms in Georgia. Do research in the library or on the Internet to learn about the many different products that can be made from peanuts.

Use Your Skills

1. What are Florida's two main crops?

2. What are Louisiana's two main crops?

3. In which states is tobacco *NOT* grown?

4. In which Southeastern states is citrus fruit grown?

5. In which states are both cattle and pigs raised?

The Midwest

The Midwest, Political

CANADA

North Dakota
★ Bismarck

South Dakota
Pierre ★

BLACK HILLS

Minnesota
Minneapolis
St. Paul

Wisconsin

Lake Superior

Wisconsin River

Lake Michigan

Lake Huron

Lake Ontario

Michigan
Lansing ★

Madison ★
Milwaukee

Detroit

Lake Erie

Cleveland

Missouri River

Iowa
Des Moines ★

Chicago

Indiana

Ohio
Columbus ★

Nebraska
Omaha
Lincoln ★

Platte River

GREAT PLAINS

Mississippi River

Illinois
Springfield ★

Wabash River

Indianapolis ★

Cincinnati

Ohio River

Kansas
Topeka ★

Kansas City
Jefferson City ★

St. Louis

Arkansas River

Missouri

OZARK PLATEAU

0   100   200 miles
0   100   200 kilometers

KEY
★ State capital
— National border
— State border

The Midwest is located in the center of the country. The region has many manufacturing centers, such as Cleveland, Detroit, and Milwaukee. But much of the land is also used for growing crops such as wheat. The Midwest is often called the nation's "breadbasket" because of the crops grown there.

Look at the map on page 35. You can see that the cities of the Midwest are connected by major highways. Some of these are interstate highways. They all help trucks transport products across the country.

 Think It Over

Find St. Louis on the map above. Based on its location, make a guess about why St. Louis is called the "Gateway to the West."

 **Your Turn Now**

As you have read, wheat is an important crop in the Midwest. Learn more about one crop other than wheat that is grown in the region. Write a paragraph about why the crop you have chosen is important.

Midwest, Major Highways

CANADA

Lake Superior

North Dakota

★ Bismarck ⑨④ Fargo

Duluth

Minnesota

Wisconsin

②⑨

South
Dakota

★ Pierre

Minneapolis
St. Paul

Green
Bay

Lake Michigan

Lake Huron

⑦⑤

Michigan

③⑤

⑨④

Rapid
City

⑨⓪

Sioux
Falls

Rochester ⑨⓪

Madison

④③

Milwaukee

⑨⑥

Lansing ★ Detroit

Flint

Lake Erie

Iowa

Cedar
Rapids

⑧⓪ Chicago

②⑨

③⑤

Gary

Cleveland

⑦①

Nebraska

Omaha
Council
Bluffs

Des
Moines

Davenport

③⑨

⑧⓪
⑨⓪

Toledo

South
Bend

⑥⑤

Ohio

⑦⑤

⑧⓪

Lincoln

Bloomington

Indiana

Columbus

⑦⓪

St.Joseph

Springfield

Indianapolis

Cincinnati

Kansas City
Topeka

⑦⓪

Kansas City
Jefferson City ★ St. Louis

Illinois

⑦⓪

⑥⑤

Kansas ①③⑤

Missouri

③⑤

④④

⑤⑦

⑤⑤

KEY

★ State capital

● Other city

⑦⓪ Interstate highway

0   100   200 miles
0   100   200 kilometers

 Use Your Skills

1. Which two interstate highways run through the capital of Minnesota?

_____

2. What interstate highway would you take to get from Kansas City to St. Louis?

_____

3. From Chicago, Illinois, you take Interstate 80 west to Lincoln, Nebraska. Which major cities do you drive through on your journey? _____

_____

_____

4. You started a trip in Bismarck, North Dakota. From there, you went east to Fargo, and then south to Sioux Falls, South Dakota. Which two highways did you take? _____

_____

5. In what city do Interstate 70 and Interstate 71 meet ?

_____

 Map It!

Looking at the map above, choose two Midwestern state capitals. Now use a marker or highlighter to trace a route you could take to travel from one city to the other one.

The Southwest

The Southwest, Political

The Southwest is made up of only four states, but it covers a huge amount of land. This area gets little rain. The Grand Canyon is located in a desert in Arizona. The Grand Canyon became a national park in 1919.

The Colorado River flows through the Grand Canyon.

Use Your Skills

1. Name the major rivers that flow through Arizona. _____

_____

2. In which state is the Sonoran Desert? _____

3. Which three Southwestern states border Mexico? _____

_____

4. Which bodies of water help form Texas's borders? _____

Native Americans in the Southwest

Native American Groups, about 1500

When the first Europeans came to America, much of the Southwest region was inhabited by Native Americans. The map on this page shows where major groups lived in the past.

Use Your Skills

1. In what present-day states did the Navajo live? _____

2. What are three Native American groups that lived in what is now Texas? _____
_____

3. Other than the Apache, name two groups that lived near the Rio Grande.
_____

Map It!

Use colored pencils to shade in the areas that were once settled by Navajo, Comanche, Osage, and Apache on the map of the Southwest on page 36. What is located in these areas today?

Your Turn Now

Learn more about one Native American group that lived in the Southwest. Make a collage of pictures that show their way of life.

The West

The West, Political

Denali is the highest peak in the United States—and in North America.

The West has the highest and lowest elevations in the United States. **Elevation** is height above or below sea level. Denali is located in Alaska. It is 20,310 feet above sea level. Death Valley, California, has an elevation of 282 feet below sea level. It is the lowest point in our country. In the map on page 39, different colors show the different ranges of elevation.

Use Your Skills

1. California borders the _____ Ocean.

2. The capital of Idaho is _____ .

3. San Diego is about _____ miles from Sacramento.

4. The four Western states that border Canada are _____ , _____ , _____ , and _____ .

5. The state of _____ is made up of several islands.

Western U.S. Elevation

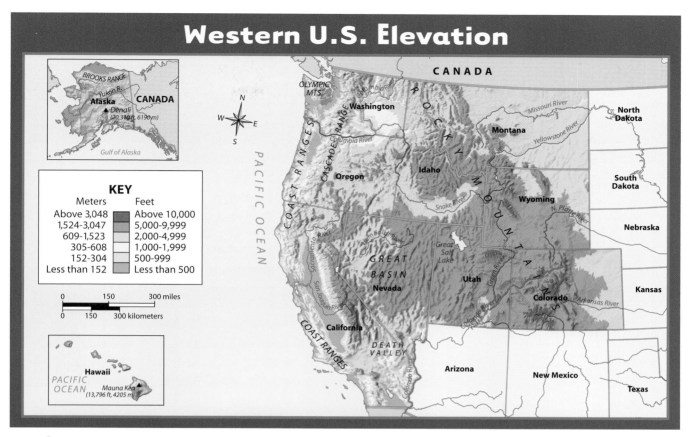

KEY

Meters	Feet
Above 3,048	Above 10,000
1,524-3,047	5,000-9,999
609-1,523	2,000-4,999
305-608	1,000-1,999
152-304	500-999
Less than 152	Less than 500

Use Your Skills

1. What state does Brooks Range stretch across? _____

2. What is the highest elevation range in Hawaii? _____

3. Compare the elevation ranges in California and Montana. Which state has more different levels of elevation?

_____

On the line, write whether each statement is *true* or *false*.

4. California is east of the Rocky Mountains. _____

5. Nevada is west of the Coast Ranges.

_____

6. The Rocky Mountains run east to west.

_____

7. The Cascade Range runs through Idaho.

_____

Death Valley is the lowest, hottest, and driest place in North America.

 ## Think It Over

How do you think Death Valley got its name?

Puerto Rico

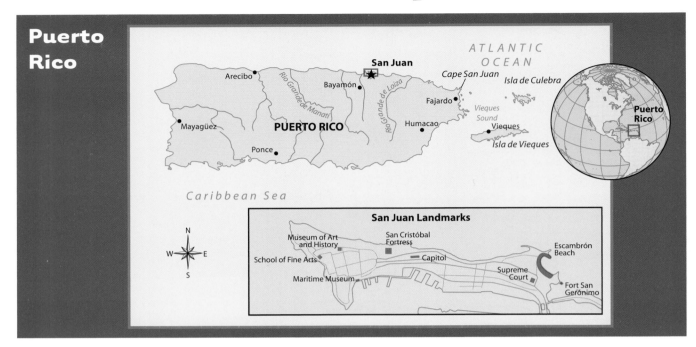

Puerto Rico

San Juan Landmarks

The island of Puerto Rico is a commonwealth of the United States. This means that Puerto Rico is not a state, but its people are U.S. citizens. San Juan is the capital and largest city of Puerto Rico. Its many historic **landmarks**, or interesting places to see, make it popular with tourists.

Luquillo Beach, Puerto Rico

 Use Your Skills

1. Puerto Rico's southern coast borders the _____ Sea.

2. Mayagüez is a city on Puerto Rico's _____ coast.

3. The Rio Grande de Loiza and the Rio Grande de Manatí flow into the _____ Ocean.

Map It!

Use the inset map of San Juan for this activity.

1. Circle in blue the landmarks where you would go to learn about the government of Puerto Rico.

2. Circle in red the landmarks where you could learn about art.

3. Circle in green the landmark where you would go to enjoy a day of swimming.

The U.S. Virgin Islands

U.S. Virgin Islands

Crown Mountain +
St. Thomas
Charlotte
★ Amalie
Cruz Bay •
Virgin Islands National Park
St. John
British Virgin Islands
ATLANTIC OCEAN

Caribbean Sea

U.S. Virgin Islands

U.S. Virgin Islands

N
W E
S

Site of landing by Christopher Columbus, 1493 ■
Buck Island
Buck Island Reef National Monument

Frederiksted •
St. Croix
• Christiansted

Charlotte Amalie is the capital of the U.S. Virgin Islands.

The U.S. Virgin Islands are made up of three large islands and 50 smaller islands in the northeastern Caribbean Sea. The U.S. Virgin Islands are a territory of the United States. The people are U.S. citizens. Temperatures on the islands range from 70° F to 90° F all year round. The climate makes it appealing to tourists.

Use Your Skills

1. The three main islands of the U.S. Virgin Islands are_____
_____.

2. On which island is Crown Mountain located?_____

3. The capital of the U.S. Virgin Islands is on which island?_____

4. The Virgin Islands National Park is on which island?_____

Your Turn Now

Tourism is important to the U.S. Virgin Islands, but agriculture and manufacturing are also key parts of the economy. Find out the main products that are grown and made on the islands.

Time Across the Country

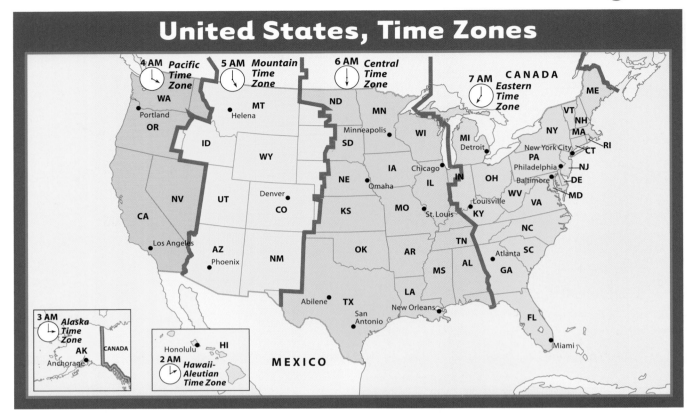

United States, Time Zones

Before the 1800s, people in different communities set their own time. When the sun appeared at its highest position in the sky, they set their clocks to noon. However, the sun reaches this point at different times in different areas. As a result, different places used different times. Even areas close to each other did not always use the same time.

This system led to confusion after the invention of railroads. Without the correct time for each place trains passed, it would be impossible to make railroad schedules. To solve this problem, a system of **standard time** was created in the late 1800s.

This new system divided the world into time zones. A **time zone** is an area that shares the same time. The time in each zone is one hour different from the ones that touch it on either side. Time zones run from pole to pole, covering the entire world. Each one measures about 15° longitude wide.

The map above shows the six different time zones in the United States. On the map, find the time zone where you live. What time is it now? It is exactly one hour earlier in the time zone to your west. It is one hour later in the time zone to your east.

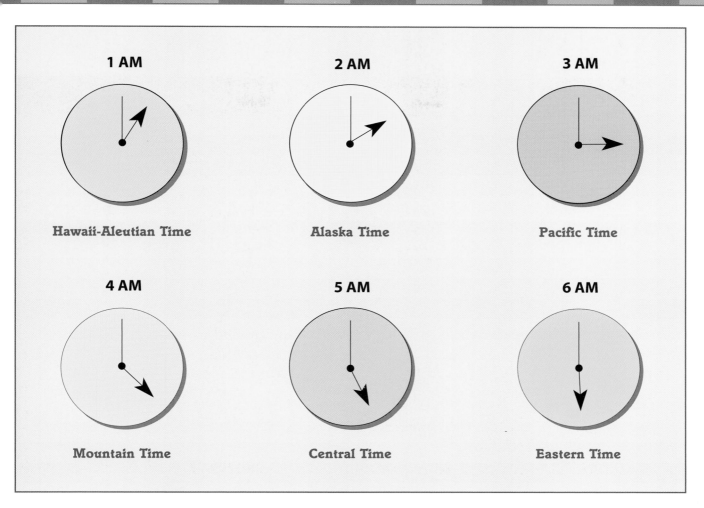

1 AM Hawaii-Aleutian Time

2 AM Alaska Time

3 AM Pacific Time

4 AM Mountain Time

5 AM Central Time

6 AM Eastern Time

 ## Use Your Skills

Use the map on page 42 and the clocks on this page to answer these questions.

1. Which time zone is Chicago in?

_____

2. What time is it in New York City when it is 3:00 p.m. in Los Angeles? _____

3. At 9:00 a.m. in Alaska, what is the time in Wisconsin? _____

4. Suppose you live in Denver. You want to call Miami when it is 3:00 p.m. there. What time would you make the call?

_____

5. What is the time difference between the Pacific Time Zone and the Central Time Zone? _____

6. Name at least one state that is partly in one time zone and partly in another.

_____

According to the map, how many states lie in two different time zones? _____

 ## Think It Over

Look at the map on page 42. Why do you think the borders of time zones are not straight lines?

Review

On this map, outline the borders of each of the five regions of the United States. Label the Northeast, Southeast, Midwest, Southwest, and West. Then label as many states and state capitals as you can. You can look back through this book for help.

Review
Compare Maps

To answer questions 1–6 below, look at the map of North America on page 16 and the map of the United States on page 27. Which map would you use to find each piece of information?

1. Which countries border Mexico

   _____

2. Whether more people live in New York or Wyoming

   _____

3. Which continent is southeast of North America

   _____

4. Which island is northeast of Canada

   _____

5. The capital city of Cuba

   _____

6. Which parts of the United States have the most people

   _____

To answer questions 7–12, look at the maps on page 47.

7. Which map shows different states?

   _____

8. Which one shows different countries?

   _____

9. What is one kind of body of water that both maps show?

   _____

10. What is one kind of body of water that is shown only on the map of Asia?

    _____

11. What is one kind that is shown only on the map of the Southeast?

    _____

12. What is one special kind of city that both maps show?

    _____

13. Choose any two maps in this book. Use this chart to list at least two ways they are alike and two ways they are different.

Similarities	Differences
1.	1.
2.	2.

Asia, Political

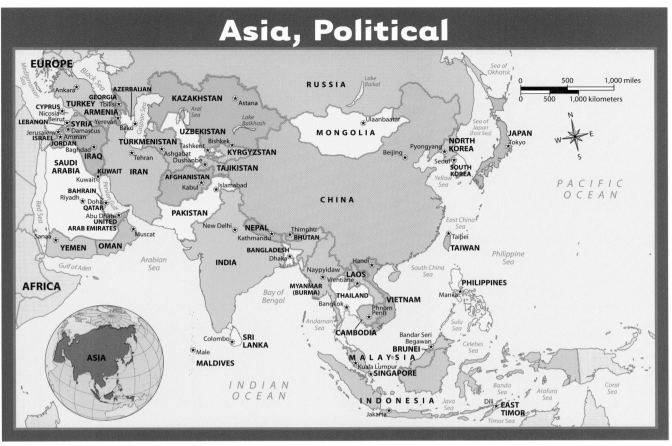

The Southeast, Political

Notes